Day and Night
at the Festival of Colors

by Allison K. Lim

Contents

Science Vocabulary

sun

The **sun** is the star that is nearest to Earth.

The **sun** gives light to Earth.

moon

The **moon** is the brightest object in the sky at night.

The **moon** is easier to see at night than it is during the day.

star

A **star** is an object in the sky that gives off light.

On a clear night, you can see **stars** in the sky.

phase

A **phase** is how the moon looks from Earth.

The moon looks different as it goes through its **phases.**

telescope

A **telescope** is a tool that makes objects in the sky look bigger and closer.

A **telescope** can help you see details on the moon.

crater

A **crater** is a dent on the moon's surface.

crater

There are many **craters** on the moon.

shadow

A **shadow** is a dark shape made when an object blocks light.

There are many **shadows** on a sunny day.

My Science Vocabulary

crater

moon

phase

shadow

star

sun

telescope

The Festival of Colors

People in India celebrate the Festival of Colors. This festival is called *Holi*.

Holi comes at the end of winter.

These boys gather to celebrate Holi, the Festival of Colors.

Winter can be cold and dark in India.
But spring is warm and colorful. The
sun shines.

sun

The **sun** is the star that is nearest
to Earth.

Grass grows and flowers bloom. Red, pink, orange, and yellow flowers grow. Holi celebrates the colors of spring.

People sell colorful spring flowers.

Holi lasts for two or more days. The festival begins at night.

Holi always starts on a full **moon**. That's when the moon looks like a circle.

moon

The **moon** is the brightest object in the sky at night.

Phases of the Moon

The moon is full as Holi begins. As days go by, the shape of the moon looks like it changes. But it doesn't change.

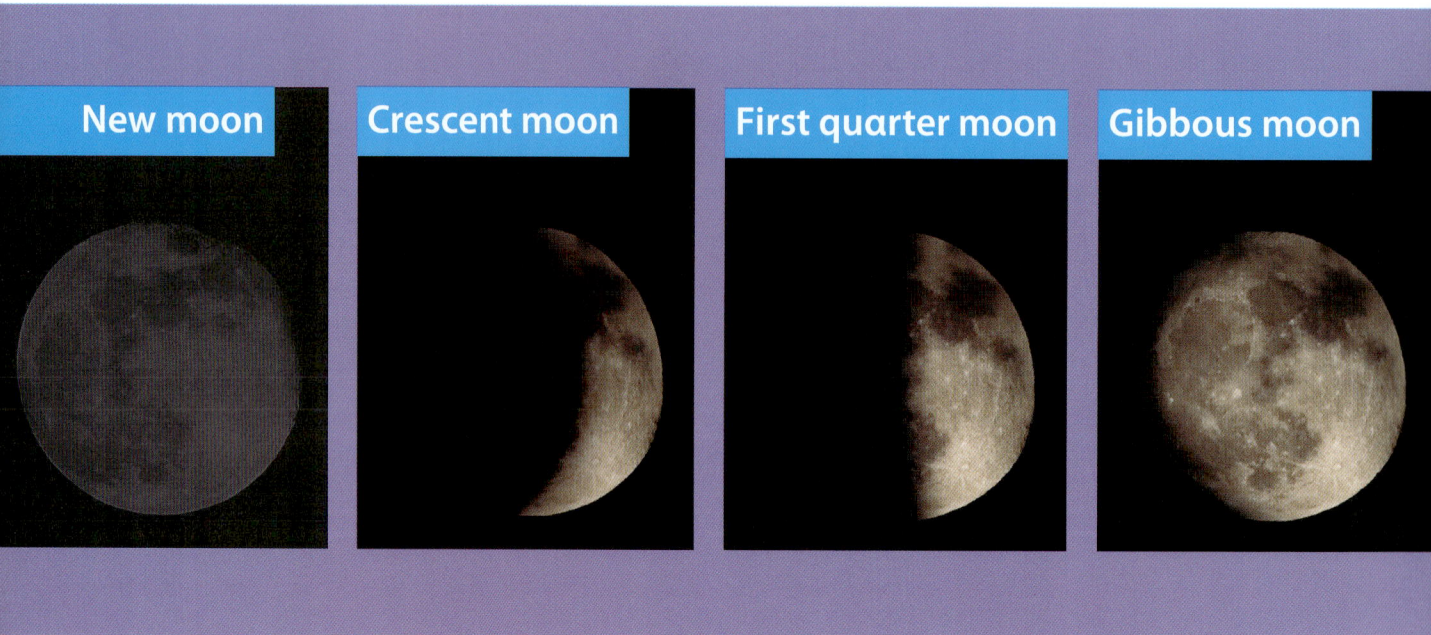

New moon

Crescent moon

First quarter moon

Gibbous moon

You see the parts of the moon that are lit by the sun. These are called **phases** of the moon.

| Full moon | Gibbous moon | Last quarter moon | Crescent moon |

phase

A **phase** is how the moon looks from Earth.

People can use a **telescope** to make the moon seem bigger.

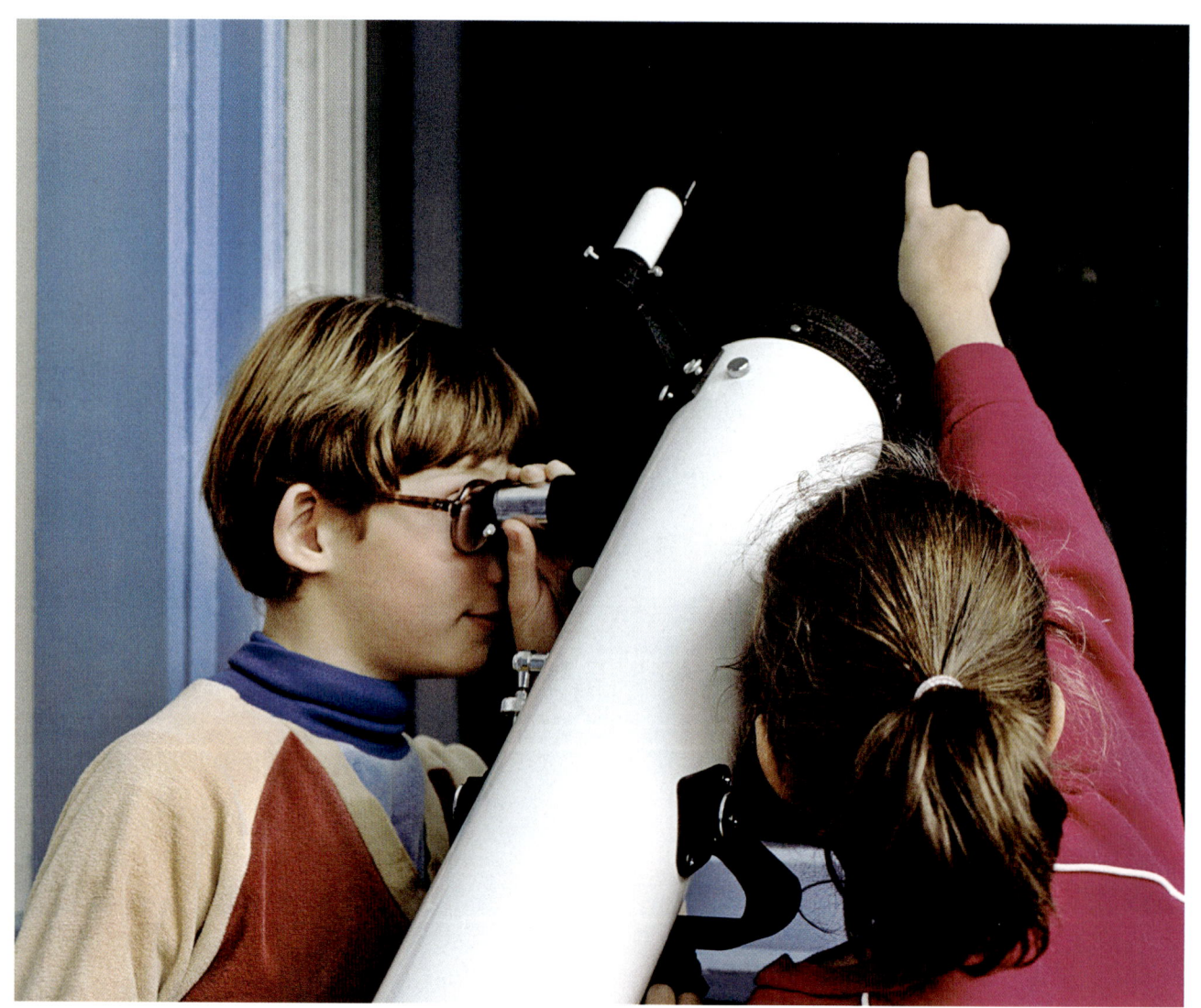

telescope

A **telescope** is a tool that makes objects in the sky look bigger and closer.

The telescope may show flat areas on the moon. It may show **craters**, too.

crater

Craters on the moon are different sizes.

crater

A **crater** is a dent on the moon's surface.

The Night Sky

There is a bonfire on the first night of Holi.

These people are celebrating Holi.

The sky is dark. Often the moon is bright. **Stars** twinkle in the sky.

star

A **star** is an object in the sky that gives off light.

Day and Night in India

Day and night happen every 24 hours.

The sky changes color during this time.

The sky is usually light during the day.

Sometimes you can see the moon during the day.

At night, the sky is usually dark.

Sometimes you can see the moon and stars at night.

The Day Sky

The sun shines during the day. Its light warms the land, water, and air.

The sun's bright light shines on the building's walls.

An elephant blocks the sun's light. It makes a **shadow** on the ground.

shadow —

shadow

A **shadow** is a dark shape made when an object blocks light.

The Colors of Holi

Colors fill the air on the second day of Holi. People grab handfuls of colored powder.

They throw the powder on one another.

They splash water on one another, too.

A man throws yellow powder on many people at once.

By the end of Holi, everything is full of color, even the children.

People have a lot of fun celebrating Holi!

Children ride a colorful elephant.

Conclusion

During Holi, the sun lights the sky in the day. Sometimes the moon is in the sky then, too. At night, the moon and stars may be seen. The moon is full when Holi begins.

Think About the Big Ideas

1. What can you see in the sky?
2. What can you observe about the sun?
3. What can you observe about the moon?

Share and Compare

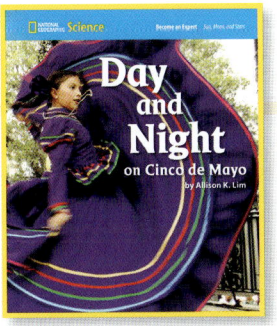 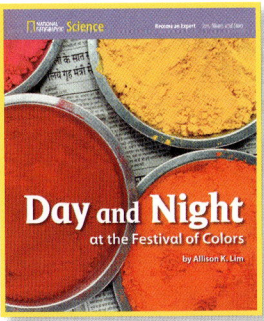 

Turn and Talk

Compare and contrast what the sky looks like during the day and at night. How is it the same? How is it different?

Read

Read your favorite page to a classmate.

Write

Write about three things you might see in the sky. Share you writing with a classmate.

Draw

Draw two phases of the moon. Share your drawing with a classmate.

Meet Madhulika Guhathakurta

Dr. Guhathakurta is a scientist. She studies the sun, moon, stars, and space.

Dr. Guhathakurta knows a lot about the sun. As a scientist, she asks questions. She learns more about the sun from special tools in space. These are called satellites.

Satellites go closer to the sun than people can. They take photos. They get new information about the sun.

Index

Acknowledgments
Grateful acknowledgment is given to the authors, artists, photographers, museums, publishers, and agents for permission to reprint copyrighted material. Every effort has been made to secure the appropriate permission. If any omissions have been made or if corrections are required, please contact the Publisher.

Photographic Credits
Cover (bg) J Marshall-Tribaleye Images/Alamy Images; Cvr Flap (t), 4 (b), 12–13, 28 Peter Netley/Alamy Images; Cvr Flap (c), 4 (t), 10 David DuChemin/Design Pics/age fotostock; Cvr Flap (b), 7 (t), 17 Science Source/Photo Researchers, Inc.; Title (bg), 21 James P. Blair/National Geographic Image Collection; 2–3 Keren Su/China Span/Alamy Images; 5, 19 PhotoStock-Israel/Alamy Images; 6 (t), 14–15 David Scheuber/Shutterstock; 6 (b), 16 Mark Antman/The Image Works, Inc.; 7 (b), 23 Jeremy Edwards/iStockphoto; 8–9 ArkReligion.com/Alamy Images; 11 Dennis Albert Richardson/Shutterstock; 18 David R. Frazier Photolibrary, Inc./Alamy Images; 20 Macduff Everton/The Image Works, Inc.; 22 Hemis/Alamy Images; 24–25 Bruno Morandi/The Image Bank/Getty Images; 25 (inset) hugh sturrock/Alamy Images; 26 Dana Ward/Shutterstock; 27 masoodrezvi/Big Stock Photo; 31 © Brella Productions; Inside Back Cover (bg) sinopictures/Peter Arnold, Inc.

Neither the Publisher nor the authors shall be liable for any damage that may be caused or sustained or result from conducting any of the activities in this publication without specifically following instructions, undertaking the activities without proper supervision, or failing to comply with the cautions contained herein.

Content Consultants
Randy L. Bell, Ph.D., Malcolm B. Butler, Ph.D., Kathy Cabe Trundle, Ph.D., Nell K. Duke, Ed.D., Judith S. Lederman, Ph.D., and David W. Moore, Ph.D.

2020 Impression
Copyright © 2011 National Geographic Learning, a Cengage Learning Company

Published as part of *National Geographic Exploring Science Through Literacy*

Previously published as *National Geographic Science: Day and Night at the Festival of Colors*

For product information and technology assistance, contact us at Customer & Sales Support, 888-915-3276

For permission to use material from this text or product, submit all requests online at www.cengage.com/permissions

Further permissions questions can be emailed to permissionrequest@cengage.com

National Geographic Learning | Cengage
1 N. State Street, Suite 900
Chicago, IL 60602

Cengage is a leading provider of customized learning solutions with employees residing in nearly 40 different countries and sales in more than 125 countries around the world. Find your local representative at **www.cengage.com**.

Visit National Geographic Learning online at **NGL.Cengage.com/school**

ISBN: 978-1-3378-7300-0

Printed in the United States of America

Print Number: 01

Print Year: 2018